INDIGO

Tanka Poetry Collection

MARIKO KITAKUBO

INDIGO: Tanka Poetry Collection

Cover photo, interior photos and calligraphy by Mariko Kitakubo

ISBN: 978-0-9915772-0-0

Published by Shabda Press
Pasadena, CA 91107
www.shabdapress.com

"The Japanese, for over a thousand years, have composed the tanka and considered it their most important form of poetry. In the nineteenth century, the spread of European poetry induced many Japanese poets to doubt that a poem in only thirty-one syllables could be anything more than the record of a momentary sensation. Ishikawa Takuboku, though famous as a rebel poet, answered the doubters, "Although a tanka may last only a second, it is a second that will not return again, no matter how long one lives. I believe that such moments are to be cherished, I do not wish to let them escape." He added somewhat cynically, "One of the few blessings that we Japanese enjoy is having the tanka."

Takuboku retained the traditional thirty-one syllables of the tanka but divided them into three lines, instead of the traditional single line, giving the form greater dramatic possibilities.

The poems of Mariko Kitakubo, both in Japanese and in English, contain a combination of the thousand year old and the most modern. Her Japanese poems have the traditional number of syllables and the English poems are divided into five lines as in tanka:

ga no kage no/ fui ni ookiku/ nari yukeri/
aragai gataki/ houyou no nochi

   suddenly
the shadow of a moth
     growing larger—

after an embrace
   difficult to resist

The Japanese poems are in ancient, not modern speech. But the division of the poems into two sections in the Japanese and five in English makes the poems seem strikingly modern. Mention of a moth, an insect appealing to English poets but shunned by Japanese poets, may seem to separate the two worlds, but the embrace brings them together."

—Donald Keene

INDIGO に寄せて

ドナルド・キーン

日本人は千年以上も前から短歌を詠んできて、その間他の詩歌が新しくできても短歌はいつも特別な地位にあった。時代が明治になると、日本の詩人の大部分が西洋の詩歌の影響を受け、三十一字しかない短歌は、瞬間的な感覚の記録以上に表現できない、と考えられるようになった。しかし、反逆者として有名だった石川啄木は、短歌を軽視した詩人たちに次のように、短歌の持つ独特の価値を伝えた。

"一生に二度とは帰って来ない命の一秒だ。おれはその一秒がいとしい。ただ逃がしてやりたくない。"

そして、啄木は幾分か皮肉に、

"歌という詩形を持っているということは、我々日本人の少ししか持たない幸福の一つだよ。"
と結論している。

啄木は伝統的な三十一字の文字数を守ったが、三行に分けて一行の長さをより自由にし、それは西洋の詩歌のように劇的な効果を生んだ。

北久保まりこのINDIGOの短歌とその英詩もまた、千年以上前の伝統と極めて新しい知覚とを合わせ持っていて、実に読み応えがあった。短歌は古今集と同じように、五、七、五、七、七の模範があり、言葉や語句の多くは現代の日本語ではなく文語である。しかし、内容は現代人の心から湧き出たものに違いない。私の特に好きな短歌は音としても印象的である。

蛾の影のふいに大きくなりゆけり抗ひがたき抱擁ののち

ga no kage no/ fui ni ookiku/ nari yukeri/
aragai gataki/ houyou no nochi

   suddenly
the shadow of a moth
      growing larger—

after an embrace
   difficult to resist

先ず、言葉が多少日常的ではないが、歌には現代的な雰囲気と感性が香っている。また、英詩の方により顕著だが、言葉や語句の間に存在する空間が多様性を感じさせる。

　最初の言葉に読者は驚くだろう。蛾という虫は歌には稀であって、蛾そのものが嫌われ避けられているが、西洋の詩では、蛾はいつも灯りを探し求めるが故、詩人にとって常に好ましく近しい存在だ。この短歌には、このような二つの意味が、同時に美しくこめられているようで忘れがたい。

—Donald Keene

"Mariko Kitakubo's sixth book of tanka is a masterpiece of disquiet and profound yearning. Its poetry speaks to the human condition in an era that has just begun to understand, and attempt to divert and remedy, a ruination that evidence shows mankind itself has inflicted on the planet. *Indigo* leaves us gazing with longing upon our own disappearance into the existential drifts of time and materiality.

Kitakubo writes, "my motherland / will be a coffin / of the stormy wind" and points to "the light rain / of radiation" to show us how "history is settling / in the bottom of the river." She sees herself as "an infinitesimal / splash in the dust" and outlines in images of stark finality a vision of sunflower seeds and a people-less planet "after the dream / of civilization." Here is poetry that steps with courage and passion into the forum of ideas and the enormous issues of our day. Kitakubo's mastery of the ancient tanka form gives to her testament in *Indigo* the perspectives of personalized history and the high art of a compelling literary tradition.

My congratulations go to Shabda Press for publishing this first edition of a work so worthy of universal value and wide readership. May the voice within us all find equal resource, principle, and kinship."

—Michael McClintock, President, Tanka Society of America (2005-2011) and author of "The Tanka Café" in *Ribbons: Tanka Society of America Journal.*

"From floating lanterns at Hiroshima to the unstoppable petal storm of cherry blossoms, Mariko Kitakubo's vivid imagery tugs at the full range of our emotions—from the horror of war to the joy of a new love, from redwood forests to dreams of Betelgeuse, *Indigo* is a highly recommended journey you will never forget."

—Deborah P. Kolodji, California Regional Coordinator, Haiku Society of America

Preface

You have not yet turned the first page of this marvelous book. Is it because snow has just fallen? Is it because your eyes are closed on a windswept beach and you feel the tide coming in? By turning the page you expose yourself to the forces of nature. You will have no choice but to leave your fingerprints on the edge of existence. This is the point of view of this book.

I have held the author's hand and stood with her before Mt. Fuji. She has shown me the voice of *uguisu,* the small bird who sings from the heart of the mountain. We have watched the clouds step aside for us to see the bare peak against the sky, and felt time stop there, shimmering.

With this book in hand, you are able to hold time in your arms like a newborn. The mystery is held back and reflected in a silver spoon on your table. A mother elephant and her child wait on the savanna for you.

This book is a personal invitation to admit you are human, fragile, ultimately ephemeral, full of desire and loss. Hints of what and who, why and where, known intimately to the poet, will pull you into confronting your mortality and sweetness.

It is no light endeavor to truly read this book. You have to hold your own life in your hands, to see your own fingerprint like a bare foot on hot desert sand. You are called by the great voice of tanka, the song it sings to you, from the delicate throat of a great traveler. She crosses borders, carrying, in the folds of her kimono, tanka seeds, subtle, perfect, potent. She will plant them in your heart. You feel the strong stems of sunflowers growing there, the natural effort, the stunning breakthrough and the ease. You will bravely open your own pen, feel ready, and at the same time, be silent. Listen. Indigo. As if the sky had penetrated the globe to the core, to invite you to fly.

Kath Abela Wilson
February 20, 2016
Pasadena, CA

Table of Contents

Betelgeuse

children
hold Easter eggs
in hands
that do not know
the stigmata

tamawarishi/ Easter egg/tsutsumi ori/
　　　　　takkei no ato wo/shiranu tenohira

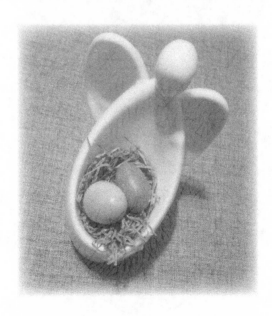

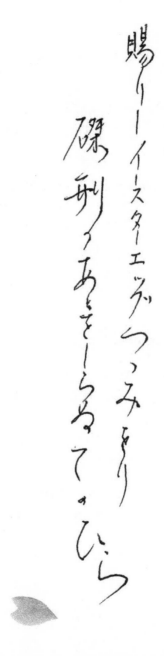

賜りしイースターエッグつつみをり磔刑のあとをしらぬてのひら

between the date
    of Hiroshima & Nagasaki

my sweat seeps
       into the small puncture hole
              where they drew my blood

Hiroshima to/Nagasaki no ki ni/hasamarete/
                    ase shimuru nari/saiketsu no ato

     oh, Yes
        they are still crying—

        Pearl Harbor
           inside of Kathy,

Hiroshima inside of me

       aa souda/Kathy no naka ni/ shinju wan/
         watashi no nakani/Hiroshima ga naku

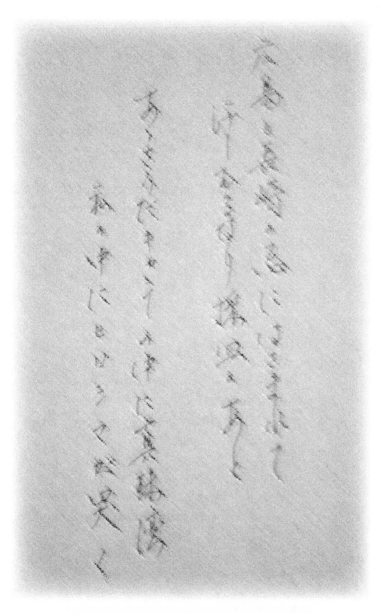

広島と長崎の忌にはさまれて汗しむるなり採血のあと

ああさうだキャシーの中に真珠湾　私の中に広島が哭く

                    footsteps
               are following me
                they bring darkness
                       from the cliff

                    at Okinawa

          Okinawa no/kano kirigishi yori/tsuki koshi ka/
               kurayami wo matoi/itaru ashioto

          floating lanterns
     on the Motoyasu river
                              in Hiroshima…
          foster Mother
               of so many bodies

          amata naru/kabane shizumuru/Motoyasu no/
               kawamo wo nazuru/tourounagashi

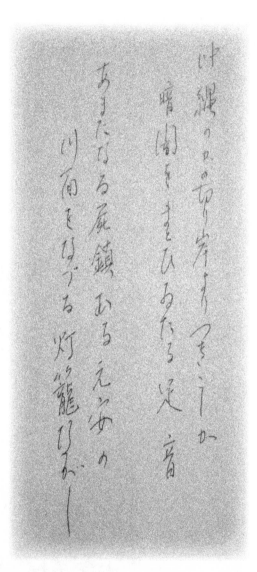

沖縄のかの切り岸よりつき来しか暗闇をまとひゐたる足音

あまたなる屍鎮むる元安の川面をなづる灯籠ながし

7

a tiny drop
 of the ancient ocean
 our story has begun …

 can you hear the lullaby
 waves are still playing now

 hajimari wa/taiko no umi no/hito shizuku
 ima mo nami ma ni/mori uta no seru

はじまりは太古の海のひとしづく今も波間に守歌のせり

cobalt blue
was my favorite
color...
until I could see it

in atomic waste

toumeina/ao wo mottomo/ konomiitsu/
genshiro naini/miraruru madewa

透明な碧をもつとも好みゐつ原子炉内に視らるるまでは

when
    will my later years
        start?—
    a mother cat has babies
        at the ruined village

bannen wa/itsu kara naramu/ haison ni/
oya neko ga ko wo/unde irunari

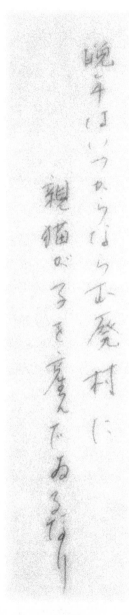

晩年はいつからならむ廃村に親猫が子を産んでゐるなり

a year later
little by little
he starts
to talk about the Tsunami,

sunset on the debris

ichinen go/potsuri potsuri to/katari somu/
kano ootsunami/gareki no yuuhi

how silent
the light rain
of radiation—

we continue searching

for his parents' bodies

after the storm,
harvest moon in a puddle
late friend
he'll be able to see this
from a cloudless sky

onaji tsuki/karemo tenkara mirudarou/
arashi no nochi no/mizu no omote ni

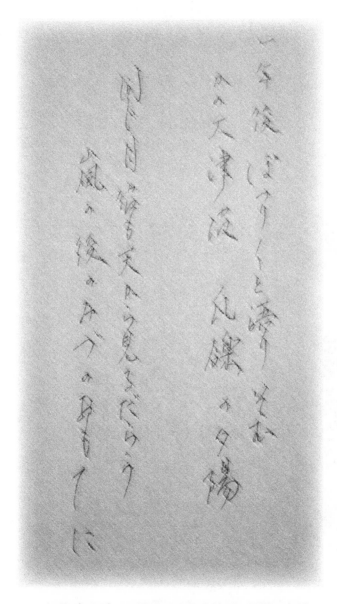

一年後ぽつりぽつりと語りそむかの大津波　瓦礫の夕陽

同じ月彼も天から見るだらう嵐の後のみづのおもてに

sounds
of the stream
in my homeland—

Strontium is soaking
into the placenta

furusato no/seseragi no ne wo /omoi itsu/
Strontium/*shimuru taiban*

古里のせせらぎの音を思ひゐつストロンチウム沁むる胎盤

dim light
of cherry blossoms—
unstoppable
petal storm in the ruins

beyond my five senses

cherry avenue
my late mother's favorite...
is there
another world?

petal drift

fukidamaru/ano atari kara/kakuriyo ka/
haha no konomishi/sakira no namiki

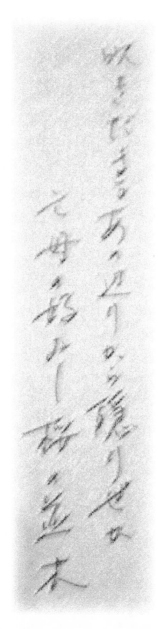

吹き溜まるあの辺りから隠り世か亡母の好みし桜の並木

emptiness
of the pigeon nest—

weak rain
makes me calm

in spite of radiation

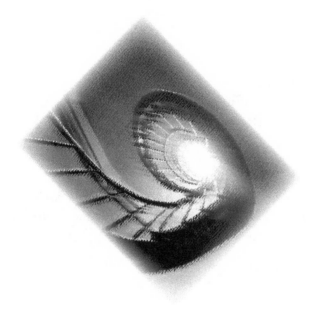

blue sky
    or mushroom clouds,

    the last view
        of our future
            Saint-Exupery

song
  of early summer—

   my motherland
     will be a coffin
     of the stormy wind

        hatsunatsu no/gaku sosogaruru/sokoku nari/
           yagate wa kaze no hitsugi to naramu

      there were
        days when I told
      my dream…

          are you there now?
            Betelgeuse

    yume nado wo/katarishi hi ari/imawa mou/
        nai kamo shirenu/Betelgeuse yo

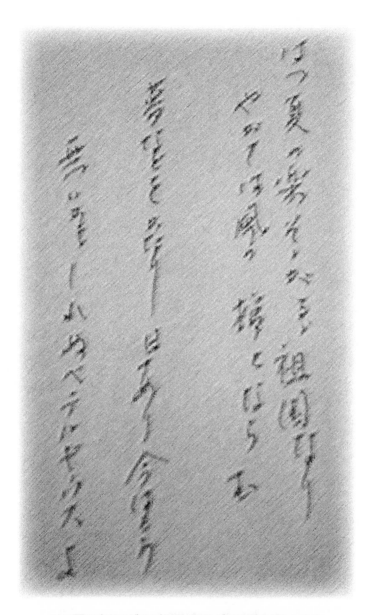

はつ夏の楽そそがるる祖国なりやがては風の棺とならむ

夢などを語りし日あり今はもう無いかも知れぬベテルギウスよ

moonless night...

    on the steps of ruin
              or into

    a kitten's milk
             falling ashes

                how like
                    babel, sullen

                thunder...
                    a blank cartridge

                    shooting wisps of clouds

down, down

    screw the staircase
  to the abyss

    tell me again how

        we became civilized

thousand years later
sunflower seeds…
may be

there are no people
on our mother planet

himawari no/tane amata nari/sennen go/
aoao toshite/ hito naki hoshi ni

向日葵の種子あまたなり千年後あをあをとしてヒト亡き星に

La Dune

at the market
among the purple grapes
a few
young green ones…

thinking about my son

aoki mi no/mazareru mama ni/urare ishi/
yamabudou futo/wagako wo omou

青き実のまざれるままに売られぬし山葡萄ふとわが子を思ふ

maybe
I can believe
in destiny—

spring rain reads
my outstretched palm

hito shizuku no/ame ni urumeru/unmei wo/
shinjitemo mimu/haru no tenohira

while
I take a nap

it descends
without the gravity

the double spiral

juuryoku wo/tokareshi jikan/madoromi ga/
nijuu rasen wo/yutayuta kudaru

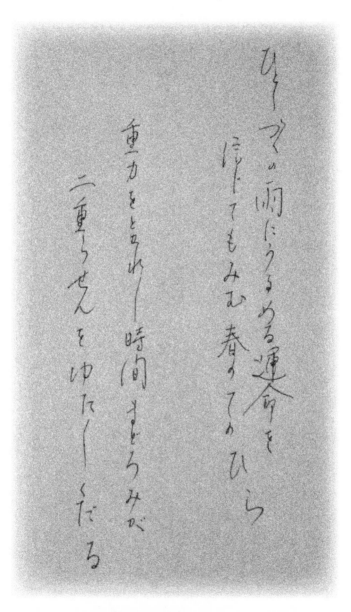

ひとしづくの雨に潤める運命を信じてもみむ　春の手のひら

重力をとかれし時間まどろみが二重螺旋をゆたゆたくだる

long sacred sleep
in the wooden drawer—

does he waken
when I wind it
great grandpa's watch

samasaruru/taenaru nemuri/sousofu no/
kaichuu dokei no/zenmai makeba

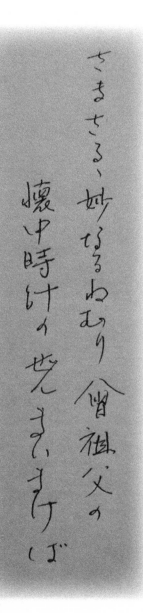

覚まさるる妙なる眠り　曾祖父の懐中時計の発条まけば

silence
       like the deep sea
          and another
        strange wave repeated

              my cardiogram

sinkai no/gotoki shizukesa/kousoku no/
nami kurikaesu/waga shindenzu

maybe
      not only one
           the time axis
              is infinity—

                Einstein is smiling

ippon ni/arazu mugen ni/aru rashiki/
        jikan jiku Ein/stein ga emu

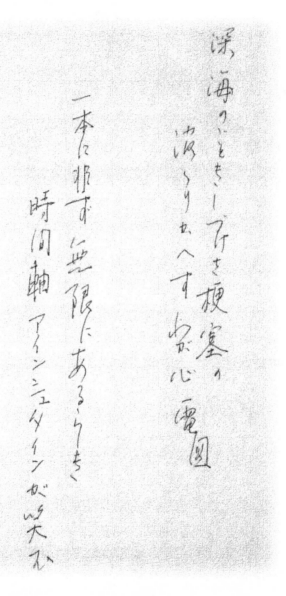

深海のごときしづけさ梗塞の波くりかへすわが心電図

一本に非ず無限に在るらしき時間軸　アインシュタインが笑む

remembering
    Father's big hand
  I'm searching
     for the ginkgo-nuts
       in my soft warm pudding

ooki teno/nukumi natsukashi/torotoro to/
* chawan no uchi ni/sagasu chichi no mi*

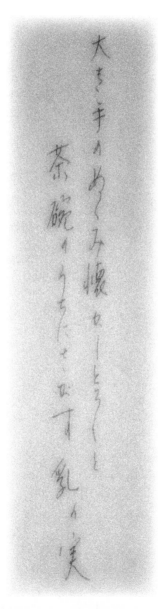

大き手の温み懐かしとろとろと茶碗の内にさがす乳の実

gone from me forever

        after so many years
           I put pine needles
               one after another
                    into ginkgo-nuts

ikiwakareshi/nochi no toshitsuki/matsu no ha ni/
       hitotsu hitotsu wo/toosu chichi no mi

the door
   is still closed—
         I, a deserted child,
        remain
           in the darkness

tozasareshi/mamanaru tobira/sono yamini/
       todomari itari/sutego naru ware

38

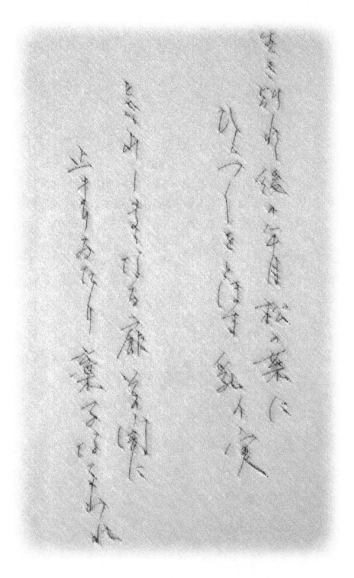

生き別れし後の年月　松の葉にひとつひとつを通す乳の実

とざされしままなる扉その闇にとどまりゐたり棄子なるわれ

after hating him
　　　　for so long, now imbued

with the longing
　　　of a child with no father

　　　　　　on Father's Day

　　nikushimi no/ato ni nijimeru/shitawashisa/
　　　　　chichi naki ko nimo/meguru chichi no hi

the warmth
　　of my father drifted away
　never to return
　　　　like smoke
　　　　　of an incense stick

　　　senkou no/kemuri no gotoku/kieyukite/
　　　　　nidoto modorazu/chichi no mukumori

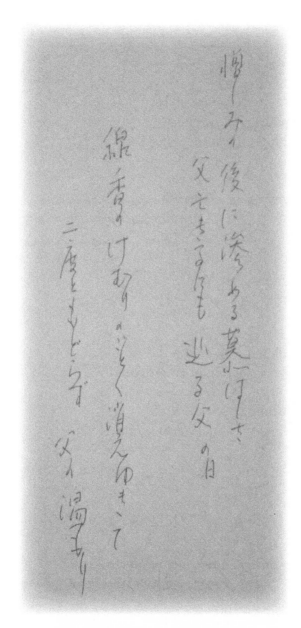

憎しみの後に滲める慕はしさ父亡き子にも巡る父の日

線香のけむりのごとく消えゆきて二度ともどらず父の温もり

even for
    a Samaritan woman
        a rain of stars

who is pouring it over her
    with the Heaven's water vase

Samaria no/onna nimo sosogu/hoshi no ame/
            taga katamukeshiya/ten no mizugame

camel colored
                sand in my collarbone

        shining
            I am also an infinitesimal

                        splash in the dust

rakuda iro no/suna wo sakotsu ni/hikarasetsu/
            waremo kasukana/daichi no himatsu

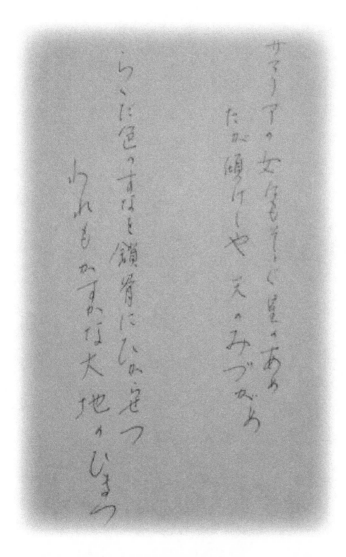

サマリアの女にも注ぐ星のあめ誰が傾けしや天のみづがめ

駱駝色の砂を鎖骨にひからせつわれも微かな大地の飛沫

ripples on the sand
    do you remember when
      you were

    a crystal rock

       long long ago

fuumon yo/oboete iruka/katsute nare/
    sekiei no kai/narishi mukashi wo

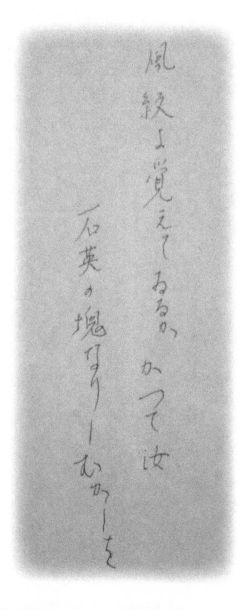

風紋よ覚えてゐるか　かつて汝石英の塊なりしむかしを

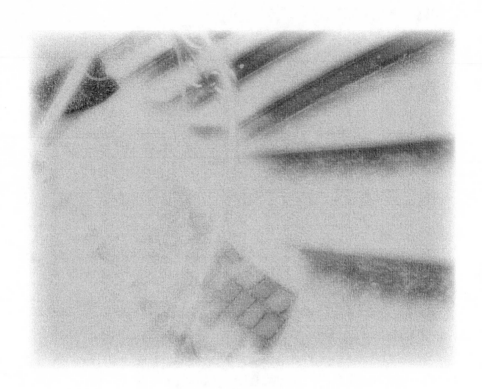

who is
counting fireflies
by the Nile?

after the dream
of civilization

bunmei no/yume no ato nari/hotarubi wo/
taga kazouru ya/Nile no kishibe

文明の夢のあとなり蛍火を誰が数ふるやナイルの岸辺

are drops
        of happiness
        joined together

by silver fingers
                behind the galaxy

seiun no/ushiro ni kakururru/saiwai no/
                shizuku tsunagu ya/gin no yubisaki

a dream
            breaking off

            just as
        to row across
                    the Egyptian sky

inezama no/yume togiretari/Egypt no/
        yozora ni fune wo/kogidasamu tote

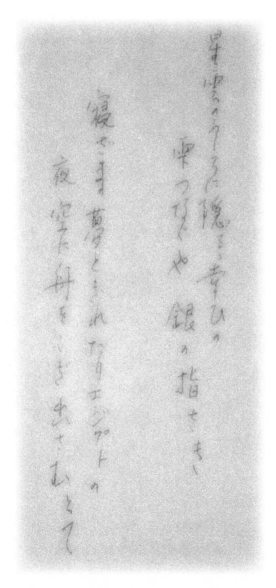

星雲のうしろに隠るる幸ひの雫つなぐや銀の指さき

寝ざまの夢とぎれたりエジプトの夜空に舟をこぎ出さむとて

over the battlefield
the moon is waning

little by little
I decay and
I lose myself, too

senjou ni/kakete yuku tsuki/kutsuru goto/
ushinai yuku wa/ware nimo nitari

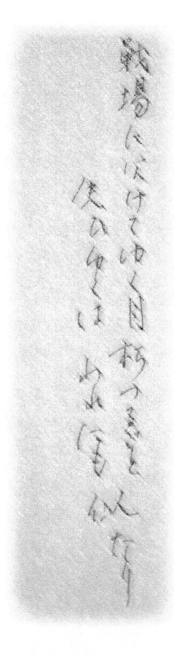

戦場に欠けてゆく月朽つるごと失ひゆくはわれにも似たり

the day
      like a common
            one—

     such a big turning point
            for my own life

tokubetsu de/naki furi wo shite/hajimarishi/
            hitohi ari nochi ni/fushime to kizuku

     as farewell
        the first snowfall—
       maybe
       my late parents watch me
            from the top of the Mt. Saentis

hatsuyuki no/wakare giwa nari/bou fubo mo/
       itadaki yorika/mamori iruramu

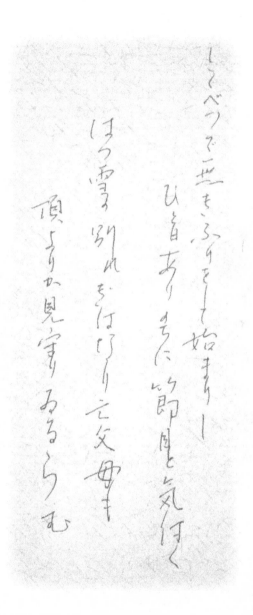

特別で無きふりをして始まりしひと日あり　のちに節目と気付く

はつ雪の別れぎはなり亡父母も頂よりか見守りゐるらむ

53

the melody
of the Galaxy—

I listen
for memories that left

with a shooting star

I balance
loneliness with
liberty—

the sky so blue
this Vernal Equinox Day

Nostalgia

...Vietnam

silent

    deep black
            soil—
dead jungle
      were gods here?

kuroguro to/tsuchi wa modaseri/karehateshi/
    mitsurin ni kami wa/itanodarouka

黒黒と土は黙せり　枯れ果てし密林に神はゐたのだらうか

Milky Way
    like a sleeping Buddha
        on the Mekong—

history is settling
        in the bottom of the river

nagasarezu/kako wa shizuminu/amanogawa/
        nehan no youni/utsuseru Mekong

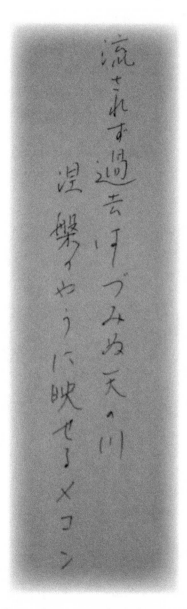

流されず過去はしづみぬ　天の川涅槃のやうに映せるメコン

Halong Bay
is the Mother of Fog

harboring
the old silver scales
of dragons

Halong wa/kiri wo umu wan/inishie no/
gin no uroko wo/dokoka ni kakusu

searching for the gods
ousted from deep forests—

karst mountain
suddenly out
of the misty sea

kaijou ni/karst sobiyu/shinrin wo/
owareshi kami wo/tazune kitareba

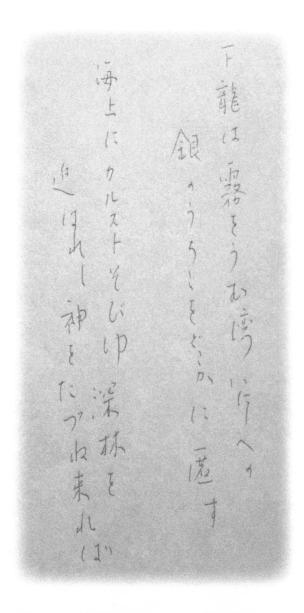

下龍(ハローン)は霧を産む湾いにしへの銀の鱗をどこかに匿す

海上にカルスト聳ゆ深林を追はれし神をたづね来れば

in the distance
        a heap
           of jackfruit
   looks like skulls

      dust on the horizon

toome niwa/toukotsu mekeru/yama uri no/
jackfruit/chihei no hokori

nostalgia—
    smoky distant view

  in the paddy
    the sandy white horns
    of a water buffalo

kyousyuu he tsuzuku enkei/suiden ni/
suna no iro seru/suigyuu no tsuno

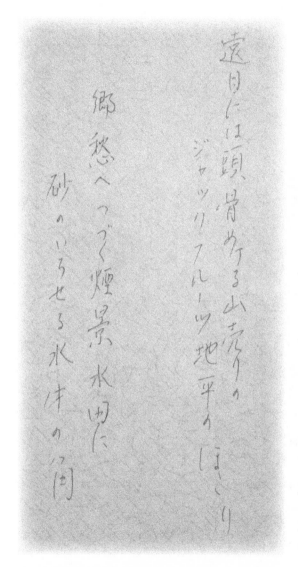

遠目には頭骨めける山売りのジャックフルーツ　地平の埃

郷愁へつづく煙景　水田に砂の色せる水牛の角

afterwards—
    his long life in Vietnam,

      duskiness
        of the ripe durian
           in his hands

sono nochi wo/nagaraeshi oi no/ryou no te ni/
durian kuraku/ureru Vietnam

64

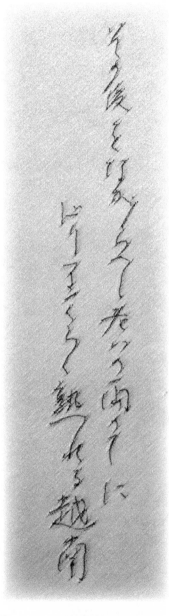

その後をながらへし老いの両の手にドリアン暗く熟れる越南

in this world
      our life
         so short

  a firefly gone and
          never returns again

sasayaka na/hitotoki naruramu/utsushiyo wa/
        kishibe ni kieshi/hotaru kaerazu

concealed
      ghosts wake up,
    a warm humidity
        descends
          on the Mekong

kakure ishi/rei ikutari ka/mezame tari/
      nuruki shitsudo ga/kawamo ni oriru

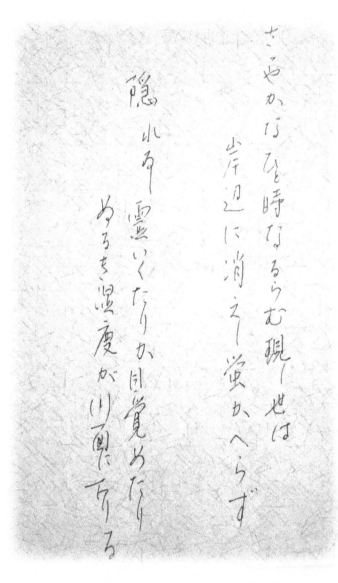

ささやかなひと時なるらむ現し世は　岸辺に消えし蛍かへらず

隠れゐし霊いくたりか目覚めたり　ぬるき湿度が川面に下りる

a firefly
        makes me feel
                nostalgic—

        I lost someone

                who was under my wings

itsukaraka/natsukashiku miyuru/hotaru nari
        waga mamoritaki/mono wo nakushite

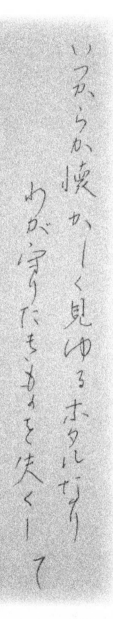

いつからか懐かしく見ゆるホタルなりわが守りたきものを失くして

im lặng
thâm đen
đất -
rừng chết
là vị thần ở đây?

sông của trời
giống như một vị Phật đang ngủ
trên sông Cửu Long -
lịch sử đang giảm xuống
xuống đáy sông

Vịnh Hạ Long
là mẹ của sương mù
chứa chấp
các vảy bạc cũ
rồng

tìm kiếm cho các vị thần
bị lật đổ từ rừng sâu -
núi đá vôi
đột nhiên ra
của biển sương mù

trong khoảng cách
một đống
trái cây mít
trông giống như nhiều hộp sọ -
bụi trên đường chân trời

nỗi nhớ -
khói xa
trong các ruộng
sừng cát trắng
của một con trâu nước

bạt ...
cuộc sống lâu dài tại Việt Nam ,
hơi đen
sầu riêng chín
trong tay

trong thế giới này
cuộc sống của chúng tôi
quá ngắn
một con đom đóm đã biến mất và
không bao giờ trở lại

giấu
ma thức dậy ,
độ ẩm ấm
xuống
trên sông Cửu Long

một con đom đóm
làm cho tôi cảm thấy
hoài cổ -
Tôi mất đi một người
người dưới đôi cánh của tôi

High tide

the color
      of Arctic aurora—
            I do hope
I'll be able to feel that
                  before the other world

yukumade ni/ichido wa mitaki/mono ya aru/
            kita no hatate no/aurora no iro

fans
      on the celling
            are turning
            in my silver spoon

                  I will miss them, too

spoon no/gin ni ukabi shi/tenjou no/
      fan mo natsukashimu/ware to naruramu

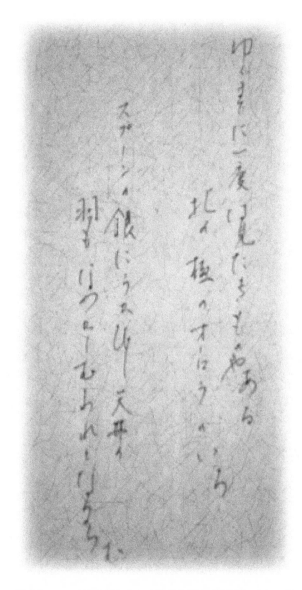

逝くまでに一度は見たきものやある北の極のオーロラの色

スプーンの銀に浮かびし天井の羽も懐かしむわれとなるらむ

five years now
since I sat there
with late mother
supping on noodles
flavored with citron

mou gonen/tatsun desune/yuzukiri no/
soba wo susureru/hahato ita seki

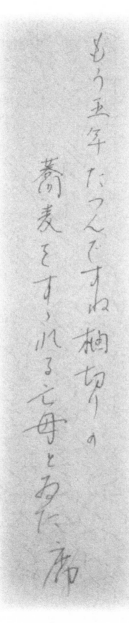

もう五年経つんですね柚切りの蕎麦をすすれる亡母とゐた席

moonlit night
in the bamboo forest

a child god
transforms into a badger
to summon his mother

gekkou ni/hitaru chikurin/doushin ga/
mujina ni bakete/haha wo yobu nari

月光にひたる竹林　童神が貉に化けて母を呼ぶなり

memories
at the Houkoku Temple—
I will miss you

silence of the wind
silence of the bamboos

kimi omou/ware to naru ramu/takedera ni
kaze fukaba/sasa no oto no sizukesa

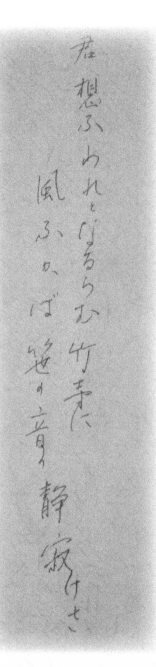

君想ふgirれとなるらむ竹寺に風ふかば笹の音の静寂けさ

from these trees
I get the spark of life
and I
gave it to them, too
in the Redwood forest

ki yori sei/atae rare ite/ware mo sei/
kini atae tari/sequoia no mori

I don't wish
to harm the forest
at dawn
the sound of mist swirling
the sound of trees sleeping

kono mori wo/ayame takunashi/akegata no/
kiri no waku oto/ki no nemuruoto

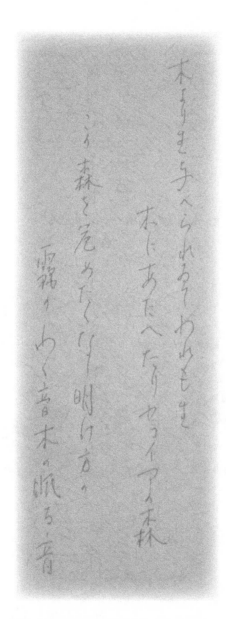

木より生与へられゐてわれも生木に与へたりセコイアの森

この森を危めたくなし　明け方の霧のわく音木の眠る音

in gratitude
      for a time of enrichment
   among the trees

       I place an oxalis flower
            reverently on the stump

uruoeru/kigi no jikan wo/arigatou/
      katabami no hana/sonaete kaeru

     raindrops
          of the constellation,
     a water clock

         sounding beyond

      an avenue of cedars

潤へる木木の時間をありがたうカタバミの花供へて帰る

pure silence…
deep sleep of Mt.Fuji,

they appear,

the forest god and
the god of water

fuji yama no/ nemuri shizukeshi/ mori no kami/
mizu no kami ra no/ tachiagari kuru

富士やまの眠りしづけし　森の神水の神らの立ち上りくる

I planted
a tender sapling
in another land…

this Christmas Bush will flourish
long after I am gone

wind, sunshine
a meadowlark's song
in the endless sky

I become invisible
at the edge of heaven

hi to kaze to/nohibari ni ware/use nikeri/
sono hateshinaki/tenngai no en

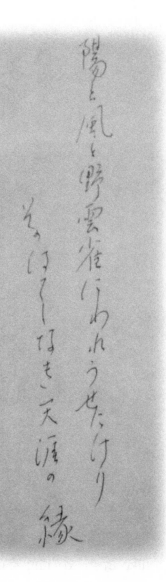

陽と風と野雲雀にВ失せにけり　その果てしなき天涯の縁

scented…
    in the forest
  sigh of

    oaks, beeches,
       larks and you

  please
    don't set out for
      your last trip…

shower of blossom
    like an approaching shadow

tsui no tabi/jitaku mesaruna/chikazukeru/
    kage no goto hana/furi some nikeri

終の旅仕度めさるな近づける影のごと花ふり初めにけり

loving you

who made
rainbows

on the bubbles
of my life

utakata no/hito no yo ni sasu/niji akari/

atae tamaishi/anata wo omou

うたかたの人の生にさす虹あかり与へ賜ひし貴方を想ふ

Autumn
high tide—

I felt
the desire in my heart
to be your lady again

kimi no teni/modoritaki kokochi/tsunori tari/
aki no ushio no/michite kitarinu

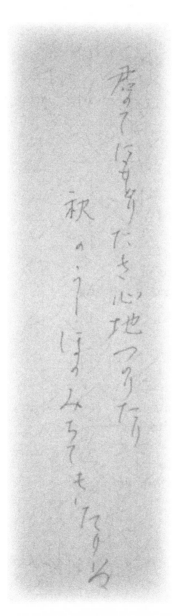

君の手にもどりたき心地つのりたり　秋の潮の満ちてきたりぬ

I'd like
    to be the mist…
        I will disappear

                after touching
                    on your chest

shadow
    of my silhouette
on the leaf mold…

      I can not accept
          the end of this love

suddenly
the shadow of a moth
        growing larger—

   after an embrace
         difficult to resist

ga no kage no/fui ni ookiku/nari yukeri/
aragai gataki/houyou no nochi

蛾の影のふいに大きくなりゆけり抗ひがたき抱擁ののち

waiting time
　　my favorite…
amaretto tea,
　　　a letter from someone,

　　　　　　　　and your velvet voice

　　　opening
　　　　　the great door
　　　　　　　of astronomy—

　　　　　　　　I close my eyes
　　　　　　　　　to hear your voice

ooinaru/tenmon no tobira/ake hanachi/
me wo tojimu kimi no/koe wo kiku tame

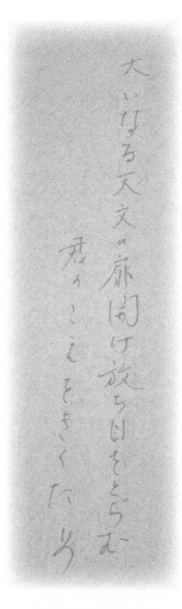

大いなる天文の扉開け放ち目を閉ぢむ君の声を聞くため

rainy day
　　　is my favorite,
one
　　　of the reason…
　　　　　moist barks are like you

amefuri ga/suki na riyuu no/hitotsu nari/
urumu jumoku wa/anata ni niteru

please keep
　　　　　my letter

it will be
　　　　my relic after
　　　　　my disappearance

雨降りが好きな理由のひとつなり潤む樹木は貴方に似てる

sound
of falling snow
scent
of firewood and baguette—

can I change my lonely life

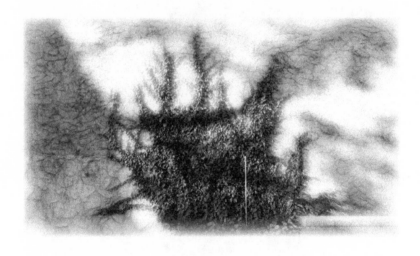

whiteness
of the lilies…
they don't need
to express their love

just stand as they are

arino mama no/sugata ni tateru/yuri no hana/
katarazu ai wo/tsutau mashiro sa

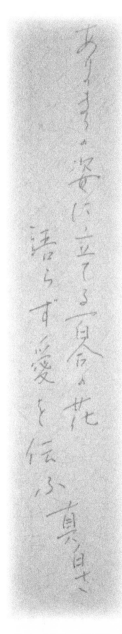

ありのままの姿に立てる百合の花語らず愛を伝ふ真白さ

I miss you

your voice
          still warm in my heart

     as I left
               from the airport
                    "take care please"

     kiwotsukete/ itte rasshai/ kuukou ni/

               kikitaru koe ga/ mada atatakai

                    the bus is bound
                         for your empty house,
                              Kashiwagaya—

          dropped off and picked up
                         the passengers

     mou daremo/ inai kashiwagaya/yuki no bus/
               hito wo oroshite/hito wo nose yuku

気を付けて行つてらつしやい　空港に聞きたる声がまだあたたかい

もう誰もゐない柏ヶ谷行きのバス　人をおろして人をのせゆく

107

still
you were alive—
that Winter

we talked a little silly
about the onion cutting

taainaki/negi no mijin/giri nadowo/
katarishi wa mada/ kimi arishi fuyu

one
after another
lilies bloom—

decorating your desk
without you, Sumi san

kazarareshi/ yuri tsugitsugi ni/ hiraki wori/
Sumi san no inai/desk no ue ni

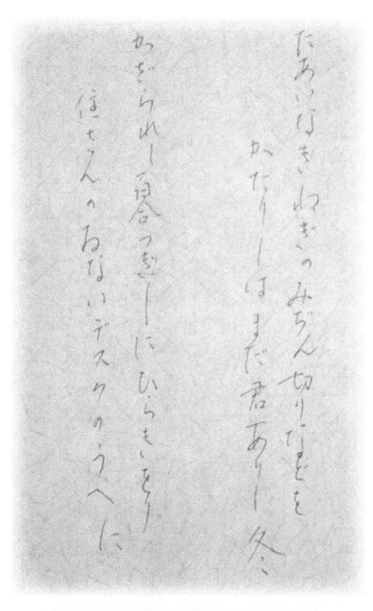

たあいなき葱のみぢん切りなどを語りしはまだ君ありし冬

飾られし百合つぎつぎにひらきをり住さんのゐないデスクの上に

109

maybe
    you will
        chide me

    if I cry—
      you passed away
                without regret, that's you

isagi yoku/ yuki taru kimi no/kimi rashisa/
                  naitara kitto/ shikaru darouna

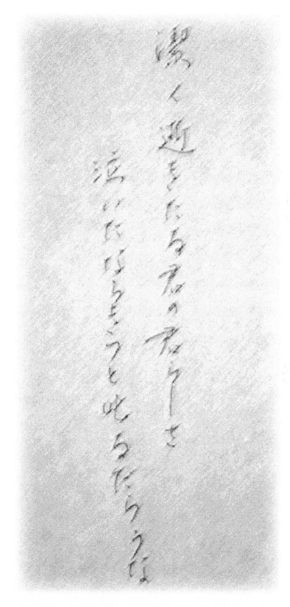

潔く逝きたる君の君らしさ　泣いたらきつと叱るだらうな

Indigo

a herd
of majesty
is coming…
in the heat of haze

elephants and their young

hitomure no/ifuu ga kochira e/yattekuru/
kagerou no naka/kozou mo majiru

I'd like to
believe in eternity—

one noon
beside the acacia tree
an elephant with a baby

eien o/shinji taku naru/acacia no/
sobani oyako no/zou wo mishi gogo

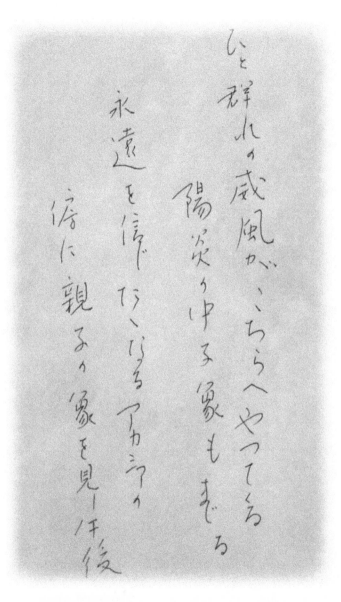

ひと群れの威風がこちらへやつてくる陽炎のなか子象もまじる

永遠を信じたくなるアカシアの傍に親子の象を視し午後

scent
of the savannah forgotten

I stand alone
in the gritty storm

of **PM2.5** pollution wind

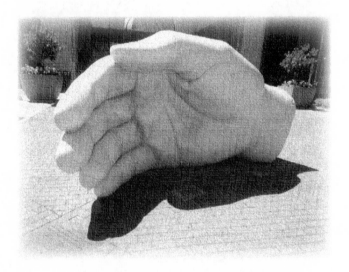

savannah no/nioi wasureshi/miwo sarasu/
PM ni ten /go no suna arashi

サバンナの匂ひ忘れし身を晒す PM2.5 の砂嵐

layers
of ancient stones

so cool
on my bare feet—

after we all cease to be…

pure indigo

settles down in my heart,
when I cross the border...

I would like to die
as a wanderer

kokkyou wo/koyuru kokoro ni/ai sumeri/
tabibito no mama/shinamu to omou

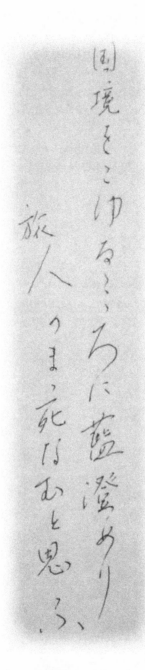

国境を超ゆるこころに藍澄めり　旅人のまま死なむと思ふ

intently flowing
the river empties
into the sea,

its mouth like a border
between life and death

isshin ni/nagarete umie/hanataruru/

seishi no kiwa no/younaru kakou

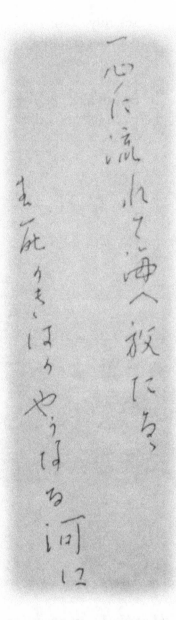

一心に流れて海へ放たるる生死のきはのやうなる河口

Acknowledgements

Firstly, I would like to say that I was filled with delight and astonishment when I found that Dr. Donald Keene gave me an endorsement for my work. I felt as if a very warm ray of light now shines upon the lonely path I have been walking.

Dr. Keene, I would like to express my profound gratitude for giving me such a great encouragement. I pray for your happiness and health. Please continue to keep watching over me.

2016 is the eleventh year since I started activities introducing Tanka overseas. Keeping in mind what I have learned in the past 10 years, without ever forgetting my feelings of appreciation, I made up my mind to continue moving forward steadily and patiently.

I also really appreciate everyone who helped me in the release of this book.

Ms. Kathabela Wilson, I am most grateful to you for your wonderful preface.

Ms. Margaret Chula, Ms. Kathabela Wilson, Ms. Beverley George, Mr. David Terelink, Ms. Kris Kondo (Kris Moon), Mr. David Rice, Mr. Robert Wilson, thank you very much for your helpful assistance and appropriate advice for the translation.

"INDIGO" could have a valuable opportunity to add the Vietnamese translation for the sequence 'NOSTALGIA…Vietnam' by Ms. Teresa Mei Chuc. Thank you, Teresa, from the bottom of my heart.

Mr. Michael McClintock and Ms. Deborah P Kolodji, thank you for accepting so readily the task of writing the blurb. I am proud to have your hearty words.

This collection is not only mine….

This is made with a lot of love from my dearest friends.

I will definitely never forget your kindness.

Yours truly,

Mariko

Mariko Kitakubo

(a tanka poet/tanka reading performer)

Born in Tokyo (4, Oct. 1959)
Living in Mitaka-city, Tokyo.

Member of
Tanka Society of America,
Eucalypt (Australian tanka journal)
Association of Contemporary Tanka Poets,
Kokoro no Hana,
Japan PEN club,
The Japan Writer's Association,
Japan Tanka Poets club,
Tanka Online Project.

URL: http://tanka.kitakubo.com/english

Mariko has published five books of tanka including two bilingual ones,
"On This Same Star" and "Cicada Forest."
She has also produced a CD of her tanka titled "Messages."

Mariko is an experienced performer who has presented her poetry
on at least 130 occasions, 80 of them overseas (Nov. 2015).
She hopes to encourage more poetry lovers worldwide to appreciate
and practice tanka.

Tanka Readings

Nov., 2015
At Ms. Kris Moon's exhibition held at Gallery Cafe George.

Oct., 2015
Four tanka reading sessions in Pasadena, California, USA - Wednesday tanka meeting, Thursday tanka meeting, Storrier Stearns Garden, and Saturday Tanaka Poetry Party.
One session Nursing Home in Santa Barbara, California, USA.

Oct., 2015
HNA Tanka Sunday in Albany, New York, USA.

Sept., 2015
Bilingual Tanka Reading at Ehemaliges Kloster Mariaberg, Rorschach, Switzerland.

Jul., 2015
Bilingual Tanka Reading at Kyoto Journal Food Issue Launch Party at Impact HUB Kyoto.

Apr., 2015
Moon Day's Reading in Pasadena, California, USA.

Apr., 2015
Tanka Reading at LanSu Chinese Garden in Portland, Oregon, USA.

Apr., 2015
Moon Day's Reading in Pasadena, California, USA.

Apr., 2015
Reading in Japanese/English/Vietnamese in Pasadena, California, USA.

Apr., 2015
Rattle Reading Series in Pasadena, California, USA.

Apr., 2015
At the reading event hosted by Ms. Deborah P.K. at "A Garden of Verses" in the Rancho Santa Ana Botanic Garden, Claremont, CA.

Nov., 2014
Bilingual Tanka Reading & Talk with Ms. M. Chula, President of TSA, in Akasaka, Tokyo.

Sept., 2014
Participated in MoonDay Reading event at Flintridge Bookstore, Flintridge, California, USA.

Sept., 2014
Garden Court, Santa Barbara, California, USA.

Sept., 2014
Reading performance event with Ms. Susan Dobay.

Sept., 2014
Moonviewing Event at Storrier Stearns Japanese Garden.

Jul., 2014
Maison du Japon, Cité Universitaire de Paris.

Jun., 2014
Reading performance with Ms. Kathabela Wilson in Tsukuba.

Jun., 2014
Poets Cafe Fan Page : KPFK Radio-LA 90.7FM on-air.

Apr., 2014
"Third Sunday Salon" at Healdsburg, California, USA.

Mar., 2014
Poets Cafe Fan Page : KPFK Radio-LA 90.7FM.

Mar., 2014
At farewell party at Ms. Kathabela Wilson.

Mar., 2014
"Garden Court" at Santa Barbara, California, USA.

Mar., 2014
"Bolton Hall Historical Museum" in Tujunga, California, USA.

Mar., 2014
"Storrier Stearns Japanese Garden" in Pasadena, California, USA.

Mar., 2014
"Taste of Japan Poets on Site".

Mar., 2014
Tanka reading and interview at "KPFK Radio-LA 90.7FM".

Mar., 2014
"Special Retirement Community in Monte Cedro" in Los Angeles, California, USA.

Sep., 2013
TANKA reading at "Center Culturel Italien", in Quartier latin, Paris, France. Reading performance in Paris in September, 2013, was my 100th Tanka reading in total, and the 50th of presentation overseas and international events. I would like to extend my sincere gratitude towards all the audience and everyone who supported me to enable this wonderful achievement. Without their support it was not possible. I would like to continue making efforts, aiming at 100 presentations overseas.

Aug., 2013
TSA "Tanka Sunday" at Long Beach, California, USA.

Aug., 2013
TANKA reading, a live broadcast, at Musashino FM.

May., 2013
TANKA reading, a live broadcast, at Musashino FM.

Mar., 2013
at Central Coast, NSW, Peninsula Community Centre, Sydney, Australia.

Mar., 2013
at Hornsby Library, Sydney, Australia.

Mar., 2013
at Roseville Wellness Group Unit 3, Sydney, Australia.

Mar., 2013
at Burnside Public Library, Adelaide.

Mar., 2013
presentation for the audience of lifelong study Philosophy Group in Adelaide.

Dec., 2012
TANKA reading at FM TAMAN radio station.

Nov., 2012
TANKA reading at the 7th International Tanka Festival 2012.

Oct., 2012
TANKA reading at the moon viewing party in the U.S.

Sep., 2012
TANKA reading at "Center Culturel Italien", in Quartier latin, Paris, France.

Aug., 2012
TANKA reading at Musashino FM.

Jun., 2012
TANKA reading at FM TAMAN radio station.

Jun., 2012
"The 16th Peace & Antiwar Festival" in Itoman-city, Okinawa, Japan.

May., 2012
TANKA reading at the Tamworth library.

May., 2012
TANKA reading at Sydney (Beecroft).

Apr., 2012
TANKA reading and photo exhibition at a charity event for the Great East Japan Earthquake reconstruction held at "Café KAZE no EKI" in Mitaka-city Tokyo.

Apr., 2012
TANKA reading at Musashino FM.

Feb., 2012
TANKA reading at FM TAMAN radio station.

Jan., 2012
TANKA reading at FM TAMAN radio station.

Nov., 2011
TANKA reading at an English Tanka workshop in San Jose, California, USA.

Oct., 2011
TANKA reading at FM TAMAN radio station.

Oct., 2011
TANKA reading at the HPNC in San Francisco, California, USA.

Oct., 2011
TANKA reading at FM TAMAN radio station.

Aug., 2011
TANKA reading at the God's HR Cafe in Australian National University.

Aug., 2011
TANKA reading at the Asian Book Room in Canberra, Australia.

Jun., 2011
TANKA reading at "the 7th World Peace Appeal with Tanka" gathering. And I appeared on FM Taman, a radio station in Okinawa, Japan.

May., 2011
TANKA reading at the Tea House Event in San Jose, California, USA.

Apr., 2011
TANKA reading at Arches Bookstore, Utah, U.S.A.

Feb., 2011
TANKA reading at poetry party hosted by "Kurenai" magazine.

Nov., 2011
TANKA reading at FM TAMAN radio station.

Feb., 2011
TANKA reading at ARIRANG cenotaph in Tokashiki Island, Okinawa, Japan.

Feb., 2011
I appeared on FM TAMAN from my house in Tokyo over the phone.

Nov., 2010
TANKA reading at "Footsteps of Basho Tour", Akasaka, Tokyo.

Oct., 2010
TANKA reading at an English-tanka workshop.

Oct., 2010
TANKA reading at San Jose, California, USA.

Aug., 2010
TANKA reading at the opening party of Tea Room Chado, Los Angeles, California, USA.

Jul., 2010
TANKA reading at Japanese American National Museum, Los Angeles, California, USA.

Jun., 2010
TANKA reading at poetry party hosted by "Kurenai" magazine.

Jun., 2010
"The 15th Peace & Antiwar Festival" in Itoman-city, Okinawa, Japan.

Jun., 2010
TANKA reading at cafe & gallery "Figaro", Okinawa, Japan.

Apr., 2010
FM Taman, a radio station in Okinawa. 4th week.

Apr., 2010
FM Taman, a radio station in Okinawa. 3rd week.

Oct., 2009
Bilingual TANKA reading at the 6th International Tanka Festival in Tokyo, Japan.

Sep., 2009
The 4th Haiku Pacific Rim "WIND OVER WATER" in Terrigal & Gosford, Australia.
TANKA reading at the following three events:
Bilingual HAIKU reading with Ms. B. George. English Haiku written by B. George/Translated by Kitakubo.
Bilingual HAIKU reading with Ms. A. Fielden. Matsuo-Basho, Kaga-no-Chiyojo.
Bilingual TANKA reading with Ms. A. Fielden. My original tanka works.

Jun., 2009
TANKA reading at poetry party hosted by "Kurenai" magazine.

Jun., 2009
Appeared on FM Taman, a radio station in Okinawa, Japan.

Jun., 2009
"The 14th Peace & Antiwar Festival" in Itoman-city, Okinawa, Japan.

Apr., 2009
Tanka reading at the HPNC jazz festival.

Mar., 2009
TANKA reading with Ms. A. Fielden at Asia Bookroom in Canberra, Australia.

Mar., 2009
TANKA reading at Ms. A. Fielden's workshop.

Mar., 2009
TANKA reading with Ms. A. Fielden at Australia National University in Canberra, Australia.

Mar., 2009
TANKA reading With Ms. B.George at Ms. Julie Thorndyke's book launch party.

Mar., 2009
TANKA reading With Ms. B.George at Gosford/Edogawa Commemorative Gardens in Sydney, Australia.

Dec., 2008
Collaboration of Tanka, Shinto Flute, Dance and Hamohn at Noh Theatre in Tokyo, Japan.

Sep., 2008
TANKA reading with Ms. Linga Galloway at Santa Monica College, Santa Monica, California, USA.

Sep., 2008
TANKA reading with Ms. Linda Galloway at Pacific Asia Museum* in Pasadena, California, USA.

Sep., 2008
"YUKI TEIKEI CONFERENCE" in Monterey, California, USA. Reading with Ms. Amelia Fielden.

Apr., 2008
TANKA reading at Temporary Rehabilitation Hospital in California, USA.

Apr., 2008
TANKA reading with Ms. Linda Galloway at Pacific Asia Museum* in Pasadena, California, USA.

Apr., 2008
TANKA reading with Ms. Linda Galloway at Santa Monica College, Santa Monica, California, USA.

Apr., 2008
TANKA reading at Haiku Poets Northern California workshop at Fort Mason in San Francisco, California, USA.

Sep., 2007
"YUKI TEIKEI CONFERENCE" at Monterey and San Francisco, California, USA.

Sep., 2007
"SEIZA WO WATARU KAZSE" reading session KIBUNYA, Nishiogikubo, Tokyo*, Japan.

Jun., 2007
"for everyone who share this same rain" at Coffee Gallery SHINE.*

May., 2007
Tanka Work shop in Sydney and Canberra, Australia.

Apr., 2007
"Haiku Pacific Rim Conference 2007.

Dec., 2006
At the English Tanka workshop in Sydney at Ms. Amelia Fielden's house.

Sep., 2006
At the workshop of first-ever Australian Tanka journal, EUCALYPT at Ms. Beverley M. George's house.

Jun., 2006
"On This Same Star" at KIBUNYA, Nishiogikubo, Tokyo*, Japan.

May., 2006
"Haiku Tanka Festival in Vancouver" Tanka reading with Ms. A. Fielden.

Nov., 2005
"South Wind at Longitude 135 Degrees East"at KIBUNYA, Nishiogikubo, Tokyo*, Japan.

Sep., 2005
At a publication party of Amelia Fielden's "Still Swimming" in Canberra , Australia

May., 2005
"WILL" reading session KIBUNYA, Nishiogikubo, Tokyo*, Japan.

Nov., 2004
"Neiro" reading at VIORON, Setagaya, Tokyo*, Japan.

May., 2004
"Droplets of Existance" at KIBUNYA, Nishiogikubo, Tokyo*, Japan.

Feb., 2004
"Ongaku-No-Kai" hosted by Ms. Takako Hasekura in Kagurazaka, Tokyo, Japan.

Jan., 2004
"Shiwa-Kai" hosted by Ms. Takako Hasekura in Ginza , Tokyo, Japan.

Dec., 2003
Year-end Gathering of "Shiwa-Kai" hosted by Ms. Takako Hasekura in Ginza , Tokyo, Japan.

Nov., 2003
Journey - Journey of Life - Gallery ALUX ARTIST IN, Ginza, Tokyo, Japan.

Aug., 2003
SAKUJITSU National Workshop at OMORI TOKYU INN, Tokyo, Japan.

Aug., 2003
Moriyama Shinto Shrine Dedication Reading Session.

Jul., 2003
POETRY INN at Gallery ALUX ARTIST IN, Ginza, Tokyo, Japan.

Jun., 2003
"Shiwa-Kai" hosted by Ms. Takako Hasekura in Ginza , Tokyo, Japan.

Mar. 2003
Flower Exhibition at Gallery ALUX ARTIST IN, Ginza, Tokyo, Japan.

Mar., 2003
Flower Exhibition "To the Sky" Radio City, Chuo FM.

Jan., 2003
Talk and Session toward Flower Exhibition at Gallery ALUX ARTIST IN, Ginza, Tokyo, Japan.

Dec., 2002
Le Petit Prince Exhibition at Gallery ALUX ARTIST IN, Ginza, Tokyo, Japan.

Oct., 2002
Boarding Ende at Gallery ALUX ARTIST IN, Ginza, Tokyo, Japan.

Aug., 2002
REKITEI Summer Poem Seminar at Kusano Shinpei Kinen-kan, Tokyo, Japan.

Jun., 2002
Marathon READING at Hama Rikyu Garden, Tokyo, Japan.

* denotes events run by Mariko Kitakubo, from the planning stages and throughout the events.